THIS BOOK BELONGS TO:

....

BECOMING
THE WNBA

BY.AHMAD K SMITH

TO ALL CHILDREN WHO LOVES SPORTS.

EVERYTHING CHANGED IN 1996 DUE TO THE GREATEST WOMEN'S OLYMPIC TEAM TO EVER EXIST.

THEY DOMINATED THE COURT, BEATING TEAMS ON AVERAGE BY 40 POINTS OR MORE.

"WE GOT NEXT," THE CAMPAIGN RANG,
THE FIRST WOMEN"S LEAGUE TOOK THE STAGE.
BACKED BY THE NBA, BUILT TO LAST,
LEAVING OTHER LEAGUES IN THE PAST.

IT INTRODUCED THREE NEW FACES OF THE LEAGUE: REBECCA LOBO, LISA LESLIE, AND SHERYL SWOOPES THE PIONEERS OF WOMEN'S HOOP.

THE HOUSTON COMETS RAN SUPREME SHERYL SWOOPES WAS THE FIRST PLAYER SIGNED IN THE LEAGUE AND THE FIRST FEMALE ATHLETE NIKE GAVE A SIGNATURE SHOE.

THE COMETS WERE EVERYONE'S FAVORITE TEAM.
FOUR STRAIGHT TITLES, AN UNSTOPPABLE REIGN.
THE FIRST WOMEN'S TEAM THE WHITE HOUSE EVER CALLED.
A DYNASTY BUILT TO STAND PROUD AND TALL.

LISA LESLIE WAS ONE OF THE GAME'S BEST, RECORDED THE FIRST DOUBLE-DOUBLE, AND WAS ALWAYS A THREAT.

THEN SUE BIRD, DIANA TAURASI, TAMIKA CATCHINGS HAD ALL ARRIVED. SUE BIRD DROPPED DIMES WITH EASE, ALL-TIME ASSIST LEADER, THAT IS SHE. TAMIKA CATCHINGS HAD THAT DEFENSIVE FEVER, SHE MADE OPPOSING PLAYERS SICK. HER DEFENSE WAS SUFFOCATING, THEY COULDN'T BREATHE WITH HER IN THEIR MIDST.

DIANA TAURASI CHANGED HOW THE GAME WAS PLAYED, THE WNBA'S ALL-TIME LEADING SCORER. SHE SCORCHED OPPONENTS WITH PURE ATTACK. YOU CAN CALL HER THE GOAT OR THE WHITE MAMBA BECAUSE KOBE NAMED HER THAT.

THEN CANDACE PARKER CAME TO DOMINATE THE GAME
ROY AND MVP IN THE SAME SEASON.
A VERSATILE PLAYER WHO COULDN'T BE STOPPED,
SHE HELPED THE SPARKS GET BACK ON TOP.

THAT WAS UNTIL MAYA MOORE CHANGED THE WHOLE WNBA STORY. SHE WON ROY AND LED THE LYNX TO CHAMPIONSHIP GLORY.

BREANNA STEWART'S GAME COMES WITH EASE. SHE"S WON AN MVP AND RING ON EVERY TEAM. SOME SAY SHE'S THE BEST SCORER THE WNBA HAS EVER SEEN.

SABRINA IONESCU, THE NEW YORK SHOW THE DUO OF HER AND BREANNA IS SO COLD. THEY HELPED THE LIBERTY CAPTURE THEIR FIRST CHAMPIONSHIP OF THEIR OWN.

ANGEL REESE AND CAITLIN CLARK HAVE BEEN BATTLING SINCE THEIR COLLEGE DAYS. THEY ROSE TO FAME IN A HISTORIC NCAA CHAMPIONSHIP GAME.

ANGEL REESE A DOUBLE-DOUBLE MACHINE, FASHION QUEEN, WITH A REEBOK SHOE DEAL AND HER OWN MCDONALD'S MEAL. WE HAVEN'T SEEN PERSONALITY IN BASKETBALL LIKE THIS SINCE SHAQUILLE O'NEAL.

NO WONDER SHE HAS SO MANY FANS,
OR MAYBE IT'S BECAUSE SHE SHOOTS LOGO THREES,
OR MAYBE BECAUSE SHE JUST GAVE US
ONE OF THE BEST ROOKIE SEASONS WE'VE EVER SEEN.
THE BABY GOAT SOME PEOPLE BELIEVE.

JUJU WATKINS ALSO WAITS FOR HER TIME TO COME. HER GAME IS SHARP, AND FUTURE IS AS BRIGHT AS THE SUN.

BUT ONE THING'S FOR CERTAIN THE WNBA HAS A GREAT HISTORY OF PLAYERS WHO PAVED THE WAY. AND AS IT CONTINUES TO EXPAND, IT'S CLEAR WE HAVE A GOLDEN ERA ON OUR HANDS.

WNBA HISTORY

THE END.

AHMAD K SMITH

WAS BORN AND RAISED IN SAINT LOUIS, MISSOURI. GROWING UP HE HAD A LOVE FOR BASKETBALL AND STORYTELLING. LATER AHMAD CHANNELED BOTH PASSIONS INTO A CAREER IN SPORTS MEDIA BROADCASTING AND MARKETING. AHMAD IS THANKFUL TO HIS FAMILY AND FRIENDS WHO HELPED HIM ALONG THE WAY AND INTENDS TO OPEN DOORS FOR THE NEXT GENERATION BEHIND HIM.

www.ingramcontent.com/pod-product-compliance
Lightning Source LLC
Chambersburg PA
CBRC090058100526
44582CB00013B/180